Cat Man Dew

and Other Poems

Mark Nwagwu

BOOKBUILDERS • EDITIONS AFRICA

Published in Ibadan, Nigeria by
BookBuilders • Editions Africa
2 Awosika Avenue, Bodija
Ibadan, Nigeria
bookbuildersafrica@yahoo.com
gsm: 0809 920 9106

CONTENTS

Part I:
Of Helen . . . The Moon Lit a Candle

I am working on this . . .

An Introductory note . . .

Ambitions, goals and careers are like visions. Therefore, in order to show you how I arrived at this stage, as a university professor, I shall start with what I wanted to do with my life in my last year in secondary school in the hope that I can convince you that my course was uncharted and that I did not burden myself with a vision God had not given me.

Certainly, I neither thought of studying in the University of Ibadan nor even considered a career in academics at all. My interest was in working with people and I first considered joining the police because my father was a policeman and I thought I could follow in his footsteps. But he had a different idea. He wanted me to be a lawyer and by the time I had finished my last year in secondary school, at Cornelia Connelly College, Uyo, I had concluded my admission procedure to study sociology at Howard University, Washington D C. I also applied to study agriculture at the School of Agriculture, Umudike in old Eastern Nigeria.

But fortune was to lead me elsewhere: my *Uncharted Course* was about to be launched. On the 8th of December 1961, I returned to Owerri for the Christmas holidays with a friend, to spend a week with my family. The next day, Saturday, December 9, 1961, my friend and I set off to the market to do some shopping. The distance to the market required that we look for transportation, and since my parents had no car, we had to take a taxi. My parents' house was located between Government College and the Police Barracks and I had two options to get a taxi—either to take the road through Government College or walk through the field between the Prison and the Police Barracks.

It was at this point that I remembered a young 'education officer', who had been introduced to me earlier in the year at a wedding. I had hoped I would run into him again. I told my friend that we should take the first option, that is, walk through Government College to get to the main road.

As luck would have it, on the way, a Volkswagen stopped, and when I looked inside the car, one of the two occupants was the very education officer I had been introduced to! They asked us where we were going, and we told them that we were on the way to the market, and they offered to take us. Then the officer asked how long my friend and I would spend in the market, and promised to be there to take us back. Indeed, when we came out of the market two hours later, they were there waiting for us! We got home, and the young man asked if he could take us to Mass the next day which was Sunday, and we said, "Yes."

This time, when he turned up, he was alone. And by the time he brought us back from Mass, I had made up my mind. I knew that I would marry this man. Imagine that, my school certificate result had not been released and I was already thinking of marriage!

Well, one thing led to another. On March 26, 1962, Mother Mary Anselm, the Principal of Cornelia Connelly

an introductory note . . .

College wrote to inform me of my success in the examination. And on June 30, 1962, the marriage did take place at St. Paul's Catholic Church, Owerri. This, you can say, was the beginning of my **Uncharted Course** and the determining factor in my choice of an academic career, because that education officer, Mark Nwagwu, who became my husband had graduated from University College, Ibadan in June, 1961. Later in 1962 we travelled to Stockholm, Sweden, where he did his Ph.D.

Three years later, in 1965, my husband (now, Dr. Mark Nwagwu) and I returned to Nigeria with our two children Ugochi, and Uzoma, who were born in Sweden.

PROFESSOR HELEN O. NWAGWU
VALEDICTORY LECTURE
UNIVERSITY OF IBADAN, MARCH 26, 2009

This work is in commemoration
of fifty years of marriage

a time is born
the moon rises at dawn
and the sun brushes her head
each hair a ray in sleepy joy
seduced by the moon's sonatas

brilliance in quiet stance
the moon curls round the sun
her cheeks resting on his whiskers
creation in symphonic celebration

time runs on
gardenias flirt with the sun
forests wrap around the moon
mark and helen twist and turn in fabled fortune
fifty years in endless dance

Mark and Helen
June 30, 1962 – June 30, 2012

A Cup of Coffee

all of life

a cup of coffee

natural beans nuggets of love

roasted beans self in furnace

crystals for brew

ready to serve

in cups of beauty

Helen

PART I

Of Helen

The Moon Lit A Candle

the moon stepped out

and held me close

i looked into her eyes

and they said to me

you will have me for ever

When you turned nineteen

seeing into dreams all of life enshrined
in an instant two hearts entwined
from nineteen forever is born
God's hand in full extension

journeys on continents adventures in daring
frozen darkness in knowledge destroyed
sixty-six lights fire retirement
it was all lit when you turned nineteen

Helen flows down

travels and journeys to places inviting
waves of passion toss hearts to the wind
winging their way seek planes skies for kisses
and i on my part dream of seas in dance

charmed winds arise float her to the shore
and Helen flows down with parachute in flood
rows to estuaries her canoe the rainbow
all of creation swim to singing colours

yellow strings pluck songs sixty eight
violins violet serenade my spirit
sax sings blues announce a new day
i walk on water hold Helen in dance

comets in fireworks compose your symphony
stars sweep down and revel in your eyes
the universe united hail happy birthday
for their special one who's ever in orbit

Your still soft eyes

i'll find you
through the lengths and breadths of this earth
i'll find you
though my eyes are bound and my legs chained
i'll find you

all i want is you

i'll move out of myself beggarly
torn shirt holed pants my shield
a being unseeable untouchable
wrapped in the symphony of your eyes

the music leads to minds unseen
the notes proclaim your grace
heard in beats of the swirling breeze
songs in solo lost to earthly meanings
a wave in flute flutters

 and i'm human again
in her home
where her hairs string my violined soul

play, then, my Valentine, play

your still soft eyes
masterpiece in song
now i have you

Ineffable joy

your margins
inaccessible
the ends are never in sight
your heights
a flight of dreams
ever rising
never surpassed
your depths

unfathomable
wisdom in vaults unsearchable
a thoughtful bubble
lifts you high
nature's masterpiece
crystal elegance

The way you talk to me

don't like it one bit the way you talk to me
turning twisting trying testing
as i learn how to walk as i learn how to talk

struck shaken smashed suffering
as i learn how to talk as i learn how to walk

beaten bruised besieged beleaguered
as i learn how to walk as i learn how to talk
harassed harried hated haunted

as i learn how to talk as i learn how to walk
where's my solace where's my rescue

confounded confused forlorn forsaken
velvety tones air my symphony

words caressing my voice resounding
i can rise and shout

i've learnt how to talk

i've learnt how to love

Your dress your address

going through the wardrobe
your clothes in quiet stance
all sorts
some i gave you and these i much adore
no address to separate them

some

you had made
Lucien the tailor

tight-fitting body-hugging
form in revelry
your figure a signature
character in ascendance
strides for recognition
and in adulation set you apart
give you a new name a new address

helenesta

bodywaves

Ibadan

Nigeria

Eyes on dome

your eyes engulf me make me
see what i'm created to be
in your eyes i see heavenly places
swirling around me reveal masked faces

eyes that drill me seeking
mined gems of my being
hold mirror to my conscience
virtues battling concupiscence

unencumbered fury in pregnant skies
rain grace-filled droplets from innocent eyes
coaxing rolling yards of vines
all this earth offers in Margaux wines

wine in soul drum to your eyes
beats magic my heart now flies
to cathedral in sockets home
built on grace in eyes on dome.

Lonely in business class

how does it happen
the warmth disappears
it's pouring rain on the outside
when did things get this way

your silken hair each strand a dream
oceanic eyes flood my soul
sands on beaches sun in the sky
guide our steps to business class
far from the coast we race to joy

your beacon eyes light the way
lead to airports out of view
for that flight our souls in trance

only one seat on the aisle my sweet
sorry love it's back to rains
i'd be lonely in business class

And i'm all for her

she serenades me colours me amber
rouses my hairs as eyelashes drum
stands above me perfumes my baldness
waiting to descend waiting to dance
the hill is steep i'm out of breath
my legs like logs shoes out of step

she serenades me sprays me with springs
from her blissful glow evening wind sings
perfumed in colours paints my spirit gold
my world in her prism i shine and i sparkle

now at her peak sets dinner for two
to celebrate our love in bites consuming
darkly she abandons me leaves me breathless
drops out of sight gone to her sleep
gathers fresh petals serenades me anew
in her morning glow

and i'm all for her

Behind you

you guide me
i follow you
i find my way

by myself
a road so clear
still i am lost...

Shoulds

you should love me
no problem
you should cook my meals
hell! problem!!

Vast seas of your mind

what do i have what do i say is really mine

and while i'm at it what does mine mean
the pen i write with the paper i write on
are they mine 'cause i paid for them

i could easily lose them leave them somewhere
and someone might find them and keep them
are they theirs because they picked them up
and somehow after cycles of finding and losing
both pen and paper might return to me

have they a story to tell me

i'll keep the story
for it is mine
it will never leave me

and if i lost some money and i got it back
would it have a story to tell me
put me to use it would say

i'm not useful to you until you spend me
exchange me for something else
i go out buy pen and paper
and write a story that i hope stays with me
but the words creep away
and like the niger coasting through the delta
find their home in vast seas of your mind

I'll dance in your eyes

find me a face

give me a smile
and i'd be fine

show me your face
seeing you smile
i'll dance in your eyes

I'm not sixteen

i'm not sixteen
wore this
to cover my age
my age is supreme
but i'm not sixteen
wore this
to cover my age

My shirt will air your soul

wearing the world in tiger-striped jacket
her eyes beam light on his vacant mind

the lecture is flowing and all is thrilled
his words as lively as her attentive smile
capture life enshrined in living
flow to minds in truth ensconced

joyful ecstatic they wine on Margaux
oblivious of news instantly mountainous
results show cancer marching in fight
the clock stops ticking time is airless

therapy in armour awaits her bride
radiation-radiant she proceeds with courage
hand in hand in morning trips faithful
salvation comes in pairs for lovers

the doctor had warned she must not perspire
and if she did to pour on the powder
wear nothing tight flowing kaftans the best
if all else fails then come in t-shirt

her blouse hugs tightly and fits
her frame like oyster to its shell

how will her body breathe and not sweat
fill the chest with green-fresh air

speechless confused his thoughts fly asunder
from Sahara to Atlantic seeking windy dryness
wonder of wonders he screams with abandon
air billowing through his scalding brain

i've got the answer there's nothing to it
from sea to sand in hundred meters dash
your coolness is tailored sewn up in a flash
the doors fly open my wardrobe revels

radiation-ready my shirts air your soul

1944

school was trauma every word a needle to the nerve

nowhere else to go school it was
class teacher the scorpion
arithmetic his venom
my seven-year mind declared i'd be ruined

how could i turn out alright

fear of sums drove me around
from mountain to valley
rolling down to unknown failures
strolling in the lowlands
energy for climbing nowhere in me
ran away from school
sought friends amongst distant trees

how could i turn out alright

the trees talked and dad heard
dragged me to school
stern strict severe his three esses
intractable intransigent intolerant his eyes
reading 'riting 'rithmetic aghast
probing pins of homework

stuck into sore bottom can't sit no more
how could i turn out right

nineteen forty-four in wanton freedom
scorpion's arithmetic ever extant
mathematics my Achilles' heel
in a mind expanding in arts and nature

i've turned out right or so i think
what makes you so sure Helen asks me
my brains in pride would answer her

'cause you fell overboard and married me

Creation anew
what a life we have

time immeasurable lost in time limited
the universe melts into a spot
. my spotless joy grows gardens uncountable
woody hibiscus nestles restful gardenias
creation anew
the universe roams in your eyes
nature's masterpiece therein swirls
colours reeling
announce their transcendence
anoint my soul render me fluid
in the streams of your eyes
speak of eternal bliss rising unseen
to heights forty eight not yet done

singing futures floating at dawn
dance our tomorrows in your ballroom eyes

Everest

won Everest in prize

in ship of floods
never been to land
on shoreless seas sail
swim yes dive too
climb a dream
top of the world must be moved
raise its head through hills of waters
then swim to buried peak
the prize is won
Helen

Wings
give me a new sky

to which i can fly
my dreams in soaring trance
engage visions
in drumming dance

The Himalaya of my being

give to me all the world
its gold its diadems
place them on the left
and on the right Helen
ask me to choose

i choose the right
except if the Himalaya
is on the left

you'd say
yes there's Himalaya indeed
and it's on the right
not the left

i see it's Helen alright
the Himalaya of my being

You now live in minds

i gave you life
you now have a life
all your own

i wrote edited published
you now live in minds
my words
in your neurons do flow

wisdom nuggets for souls
seeking new faith
in African truths

Poetic joy

they say
if a wife is good
the husband
happily sails through life

if bad
her man
translates monstrosity
to poetic delights

wife's evil beguiling
makes him spin words
on beds of venom
bitterness sewn into blanched sheets

we come in various hues
red and outlandish
orange monsters
green heroes
bodies unrevealing
eyes unsearching

we create our own monsters
emeralds to soapstones
blow them far off
to forlorn despair
steeped in loveless life
the wifely poet reads syllables
off the tongues of mindless gods

no consonants no meaning

poetic joy lives
in transcendental pain
transforms life's peccadillo
into frolicking mirth

bad wife good wife
in dance

Creation shore
assembled in the hall

suit and tie in union
air streams round you
finds my barren eyes sternness
is bathed in love perfumed

my soul at peace
rows on its oars
words sublime coax minds in storm
your searching face finds passage
to creation shore

Glaciers of joy

how do i say thank you
one greater than the next
where are the limits to joy
the margins expansive

where in my heart are spaces
for the glaciers of joy rushing from your soul
the parched desert of my being
can't drink enough of your oceanic eyes

where are the boundaries of joy
ever stroking the whiskers of angels
in resounding praise and jubilation
beating heaven's drums in adulation

lucky me
for all this is mine
in you i'm transformed
in you i breathe

What of love

Everest thrusts its head
eight thousand metres of earthly crown
still it has a peak and higher no more

what of love
you love me as i never expected to be loved

give yourself selflessly embedded in my soul
yet there is space unfilled
heights without tops
beyond Himalayan skies

body and soul yearn for more
but don't know what more is
how described
mystery unto self

i give you love no limits
in words in rhythm in music
all day long the drums beat and
singing strings play your tunes
even new tunes unplayed before
i stretch my hand east to west

and back
to clasp you
surround you
feast on your eyes
sweet juices of my soul

lift you to topless towers on
beaches of gracious frolic
search the universe with
beaming light
of your boundless eyes
to give you a pure
diadem of crystal joy

and you say there must be more
and you don't tell me what more is
or how described

i'll climb Everest and from the top
stride to your beckoning
ever challenging
as i enter new orbits of celestial love
to find this more

Your face was not in the cup

the night was rough

your insides in revolt
with you getting up
now and again
to attend to unknown results
of dietary indiscretion

morning
you're still lying there
knees pulled to chest
duvet spilled on the floor

i stepped out
made me some coffee
but it just wasn't the same
'cause your face
was not in the cup

The joy of your eyes

you are my past
here we are engulfed in each other
thoughts float off our minds
spread their wings an umbrella
for our memories keep them readied
for easy recall of what the past is

you were only nineteen fresh from school
and i a little hardier from years at college
still green and unsullied
filled with dreams
of a life only that damsel would grant

her skin supple
limbs forever in dance
in roaring laughter in a world of grace

and who could she be
my future blasting in my past

you come along
dreams undreamt
make me fly higher and higher
no tops unreachable
to the joy of your eyes
nature's masterpiece revealed
redemption magnified

now where were we

no we don't have a past

you are mine and i yours
life eternal in your eyes
the heavens proclaim

You're a place

you're a place
when
i'm with you
i've reached
my destination
place person time

all wrapped in you

Unstoppable tide

you're unstoppable tide
runs to the estuaries of my desires
the rivers of my blood
my spirit in flood

my dreams turn to dust
in the glare of your eyes
your laughter gamely fills
the marrow of my bones

your tides ever rising
create fresh rivulets
the virgins of my dreams
of a valentine epiphany

The feast of your eyes

if you're a hill how do i climb you
to gain your top in cloudless skies
gather you in my weighty arms
strengthened by your urgent buds
weakness transformed as i embrace the ladder
each rung a flower of your spring-time blossoms

limbs astir hips heaving
joys glitter guide my way
lighting your diadem of purest jewels
our marriage mined in bottomless bliss

the journey untiresome each step a reward
worth all my energies a gift of the gods
for a husband in ascent to dreams undreamt

and now at the top to take you home
to that uncooked meal for salad-loving hearts
a gentle wind rustles through the sheets
my marrows dance to the feast of your eyes

Mere words

large huge monumental
mere words
human heart beats them all
rises above in mysteries
there written
by one soul deciphered
love an ocean surrounds the soul
floats my heart
bears me where you go

large huge mountainous
mere words
a grain of sand on the seashore
not lonely lying there
amidst millions others
yet a complete being itself
the universe there enwrapped
in uniqueness
my heart a grain of sand
in your eternal shore

Absence distance

gone from me

she's absent
here i am
mov'd to write

words fill the space
of her lively mind
render'd on paper
held in my hand

no longer distant
here present

Last night

you came to us
told us
how much you loved us
the way we live
the way we are

the titanic
ship of dreams the world afloat
wealth weaves threads of gold
around needing necks
dinners and dances wines and liqueur
lounging and swimming
fine clothes and furnishings
sleeping on satins

all upstairs

in the bottoms
music and mellowing smoking and shouting
noise rising in heated arguments
talk and more talk rambunctious
gaiety in gallons washes torn jeans
folds rumpled blouses
joy in pursuit paints faces in rainbow dance
loving poverty pounds the floor
delight drugs the soul
all downstairs

leaky roof ants and rats

he lumbers in

moves mattress to the dry floor
lies to rest
raises head to the Himalayas
of heaven's pillows
from upstairs Helen descends

keeps him warm melts the snow
laughter flows down her cheeks
gold in a furnace
burns up pride in sultry state
nuggets burnished in purity
soul necklaced in jewelled joy
and downstairs serenades upstairs

mud to Everest rises
twines of rain gird the sea
eyes surge and ears stroll
lips in song confirm mystery's text
in us transfixed

now you know
the way we are

Vote Rivers president

forests blow trumpets
and green fields triumph

i watched you today
come toward the gate
in longsleev'd blouse
ankle-length skirt
flared flowered flowing
your head held high on
pedestalled neck
to cast your vote
for your Rivers president

you swayed swinging
your gait a thrill
you danced to the flutter
of the bougainvillea petals
feet floating in the air
buoyed in freedom
face aglow with morning sun

the sands ambled
to be stepped upon
each grain beats the other
to grant you poise

Obetiti* in gloom
frangipani fragrance
flares your flambé eyes

*village in Nguru, Aboh-Mbaise LGA, Imo State.

The curled heavens of your lips

if you were the road

and i a car
how would i drive

my tyres my heart
ever running
and you with a firm grip
steer my soul

i speed and
you ask why where to
when you're spread out
from east to west
to places i've never reached

racing to encompass you
you tell me still
there's more to know
places to go
what of the skies above your heart

spread your wings all over me
i plead from road to sky
i'd have to fly
leave car
i will ascend
grow massive wings
enlarge my heart
for greater speed all pistons firing
for this new journey
into unsearchable heights

wondering what lies west of me
your unfathomable treasures
there encased
awaiting release
to flood my arid soul

i swim in the air
descend from above
where skies stir your eagle eyes
and my car can race forever
on the curved heavens of your lips

Helen (because of nature)

nature

incongruous confounding
simple reachable
never ending
a journey for astronauts
ever rising
your depths unfathomable

wisdom alive in vaults unsearchable
tiny bubbles float to the surface
our intellect their resting place
deeply penetrating knowledge enriched
now enter Helen

in nature onion grown
beauty inexhaustible in each peel
your margins spread far out

we reach the ends and discover
fresh expanses await us

Scraps of love

are love letters written

on scraps of paper
avow all the world has
to one refined and pure
raining dews of mirthful ease
revive heart eager for words

a scrap of paper is all i have
the words minted in pulp's furnace
zest blazoned in white
for one who clasps me won't let go

Who cares

who cares
head boils
thoughts distilled
seeking symmetry
one or two well formed
emerge
written down
all of life's best
minted in words
formation revealed

In the streams of your eyes

what a life we have
time immeasurable in times so limited
and all the earth melts into a spot
my spotless joy grows gardens uncountable
woody hibiscus nestles gardenias
creation anew
the universe

basks in your eyes
nature's masterpiece swirls therein
the rainbow in dance adorns your brow
drums triumphant leap on your eyelids
anoint my soul
render me fluid
in the streams of your eyes
whispering years streak in your eyes

speak of eternal bliss rising unseen
forty eight laps in life's endless track
still it's morning in your morning eyes

Waiting for Helen

parched earth crackling
cracked skin stretched for drumming

soul on desert waiting for rains
of swanny eyes

clouds flutter as wind whistles
they touch land rivers of joy

and Helen floats down
fluids my soul

What about now...

could pride myself
my tummy a quarry
crunches bones into succulent joy
what about now

my tummy a furnace
burns up yams and stockfish
revels in charcoaled peace
what about now
all things hot all things cold

watered my tummy
made it a forest feast
what about now
beans and rice and melons and peppers

mixing turning churning grinding
my tummy dancing on fluid foundation
what about now
throwing up whirling round

my head in vertigo i'm near dead
but not quite
you come to me and give me a smile
tummy's back to service
my head now can think

The game

Helen is blowing things out of proportion

i too am blowing things out of proportion

come Lord be the referee
blow your whistle

and get the game back on track

A prism of joy

your innocence grounded in beauty

germinates gardenias in bloom
all of nature in dazzling prisms
bathes your face in rainbow diamonds

in a cup of coffee

every morning
you bring me
a cup of coffee

a moment
a heartbeat
brewed love
in your hands

a cup of coffee
canvas for painting
brush strokes eternal
re-create
your flowing eyes

brown beans brew
our minds flow
form purity crystals
in a cup of coffee

orbital eyes

her eyes serene sincere
invite trust confidence
endow her
with qualities sublime
recall memories of self to me
make me wonder
what can i offer her

her eyes deep distant
invite silence meditation
endow her
with qualities restful
recall memories merely formal
make me wonder
if i can be sombre

her eyes bold brave
invite fortitude assurance
endow her with qualities trustful
recall memories of fidelity
make me wonder
if my soul is stout

your eyes fragrant a festival
invite strings and songs
endow you with qualities symphonic

recall memories revolving in joy
make me wonder
if i'm in your orbit

any which way

you and i are this way
horizontally
you and i are this way
perpendicularly
you and i are this way
circularly
you and i are this way
on-line
you and i are this way
off-line
you and i are this way
native
you and i are this way

brownskinned

.

Looking at you

sat there looking at you

my heart on a boat on the sea-filled room
each beat an oar stroke in pulsating speed
to palaces of your crystal eyes

lost
can't contain the joy
one room beckons then another
confounded i saunter
meander
your invitation makes me surrender

i yield all i am
to gain all you are
mingled our bloods eternal
form seas overflowing

my weary oars in your eyes find new strengths
on to victory i row to that unknowable
yet known
island you created
only for my soul

Worse makes better

my husband has grown worse
over the years
and i in result
have become better

Married fingers

don't have to dig deep
bottom's lifting
all's about
in sands transcending

joys in baskets proudly basking
toil and sweat sweeping through
beating drums dripping bubbles

frozen prism princely reflecting
married fingers ringed in rainbows
all's on top in kingdoms of being

In your smiling eyes

let me ascend to you
clothe my dreams
warmth therein
wake them up
grant them sinews
render me sublime
in your smiling eyes

a Kathmandu Christmas

in flight with Helen all over the world
from Obetiti to Ontario and places far out
to Kathmandu from vineyards by Niagra on-the-
Lake
to Bethlehem Christmas eternal
to adore the Infant Jesus our wines for Joseph and
Mary
our love sealed in everlasting peace

To say

to say i'm bored

is to say
i don't love you

A time for (h) earring

horns and drums and strings and sax
tenor and bass and all sublime
songs stir air and beg to fax
phoned to strings in dropp they chime
pen-du-lum of dropp ear- rings
obeying neck and shoulder swings
phone time to ears and heaven sings

To singing colours swim

journeys to places inviting
waves of passion toss hearts to the wind
winging their way
planes seek skies for kisses
i dream of seas in dance

charmed winds arise float her to shore
Helen flows down liquefies the flood
rows to estuaries her canoe the rainbow
all of creation swims to singing colours

yellow strings strum play songs sixty eight
violins violet serenade my spirit
the sax sings blues announce a new day
i walk on water tango with Helen
comets in fireworks compose their symphony

stars sweep down revel in your eyes
planets hail happy birthday
for their special one who dazzles the sun

Life

torn
ripped apart
life
tell us who we are

megastars
heavens open
genius raining
songs flood hearts
life re-created
on stage

within the soul a stranger
seeking revelation
life mystery
teach us to live you

strong on stage
fragile at heart
fruits surpassing
promise of the flowers
in God's embrace

life

I'm not sixteen

i'm not sixteen
wore this
to cover my age
my age is supreme
but i'm not sixteen
wore this
to cover my age

Little things

the look of things does it matter

eyes see things as they are
more still more
discerning eyes see
God's design in little things

Can't see my eyes

i cannot see my own eyes

things outside of me
i can see love enjoy
but the eyes that see them
i cannot see

created for others not ourselves
it's our response to what we see
in the other that defines us
makes us see into our own eyes

Angels of joy sit on my brow

angels of joy sit on my brow
pour in light each ray a thrill
my spirit rises the heights unseen
colours assemble invite the rainbow

dazzling prisms flash over me
diamonds radiant incense the soul
grace exults learns a new song

to reach that heart too sublime for letters
for only the Word would do
the soul tingles with dreaming scratches

heaven drops in seeks out some drums
saints in dance create a new earth

Wood transformed
seeking fulfilment

i pierced your side
my sins the spear
don't want your blood

to run aground i drink it all
i hammered your feet

to the wood my sins
the nail
don't want the blood

to run aground
i place a pan under your feet

collect the flow
i bear the pan

on my head
won't let it spill
nailed your hands

to unyielding tree
shorn of leaves
my sins the blow

don't want the blood
to run aground
i spread my palms to meet yours

your arms spread out

wood transformed
my saving Cross

now
you cover me
in and out and in again

Duty to beauty

God's creation all marvellous
fill us with wonders at works supreme
we behold it all seems confusing
far beyond reason seeking understanding
the mind in quest cannot fathom all there is
the human person the greatest wonder of all

beauty on duty

mountains rise into skies above the earth
life cannot subsist birds cannot perch
why mountains what purpose do you serve
only a few can climb in pain
courage is lifted patience rains down
the brave go up held on ropes of hope
desire towers pumps the heart weakness slithers
many find their mettle still well steeled
would rather dwell on worthy matters
where the world lives and birds beat the air

duty to beauty

what of the planets living their orbits
each oblivious of the other no handshakes here
won't fall or run into the other no show of love
around and around they swirl in fulfilment
doing God's work in obedience to physics
human knowledge comes to the rescue
introduces bodies to others summoned to dinner
humans form friendships with planets in palace

mountains and moons jollying on Mars wake up for
breakfast
all revel in God's buffets revealed in grace
beauty to duty

all God's works are beauty in his eyes
all to his glory or they would be unmade
corruption announces senators selection for elective
eyes
lights from lamps lit by greed by lust by pride
sights disfigured by mind's creation grey sands for
shores
constructions designed on faulty knowledge
errors shroud images sublime beauty occluded
beauty cries to duty

mountains rise above our heads lift our vision

heights beyond conception inflame the spirit
enlarge our lives give us huge hearts in priestly
training
life transformed transcends experience spirit in fury
grow and burst whatever's in chains
nature charges beckons soul to journey eternal
bring your tents people bring your evils
with each step shelter unfolds larger and larger
bears us to the top – crash, tents are punctured
stones and shrubs resist evil pierces our cover

down we fall build new nests for eggs of good
to hatch on valleys of grace and virtue is born
warm air descends our babies noble cry in joy
duty to beauty

vastness veers shores unseen eyes impeded

oceans roar friendly waters command willing ships
to set sail continents undiscovered flash their lights
fishes flip line up in salute
ships to sink new faces to devour ere they reach
shores
to ocean floor condemned their meats consumed
all the sharks dart and dance in transient conquest
not browbeaten humans excel new continents their
prize
the glory of God is humans alive
duty to beauty

Always with you

i always wish to be with you
spend time with you

doing ordinary things
cut your hair just the growing tips

cut your nails wash your clothes
hang them to dry
clean the sand off your sandals
what else can i do for you

perhaps boil water for your bath

(or are your baths cold)
make *eba* give you *ofe owerri*
wash the dishes after you've eaten
stitch your torn togas iron out the wrinkles

soak your feet in soapy water dry them off
trim your moustache watch you smile
all this i'd do if I lived with you

in desert Nazareth
and you what do you want of me

you tell me go to Mass and there
drink you in wine
silent fluid for splendid souls
fill me with forgiven pride
clasp your breaded body in my bones
read the scriptures see through your eyes

as i ponder the mystery that made me

smile in my anger as you slip and fall

your strength in sin as you raise me up
be patient when you come to my house
and before you sleep just roll over me

It's all clay

plates saucers dishes

vessels of clay
can't collect my blood

find something permanent
bronze silver even gold
can't help it Lord

it's all clay in my bones
even in my hair
just as you made me
forgive me i pray
it's all clay

Iwollo*

you stand there watchful
and i in awe offer praise

tall and solid you're steadfast
nature at work over creation

lowly grass velvet spread
feast for the eyes supple to walk on
master of beauty green of compassion
ever willing offering self
we cut down tress clear all growth

 leave you standing in hearing distance
contrite in love we sing your valour
you flap your ears grant us forgiveness

* *Iwollo, a town in Enugu State, Nigeria*

Leaving Iwollo

leaving you where you are
i take you with me as I go
others will come and hold on to you

you in me will grow and spread
i'll come back and grasp you

solid wood tender pulp
firm embrace encircling love

Mow me down

i am nothing let me be nothing

make my nothingness yours
dispossessed naked infirm
cut me low let me be
that you may walk on sin
step on me lie and rest
make me low spread on me
i'll grow flowers

and make you smile

Skies of rainbowed virtue

two worlds in fresh creation

helices of joy the soul circling
magnify all that is worthy

girdle the spirit
seek a new existence
in souls soaring to skies
of rainbowed virtue
heavens emerge from friendship

hatched in Pauline bliss
boundless seas drown shifty shores
lift up islands endless in love

Of salty pain
the cross triumphant of salty pain

wooden pole seeped in weeping blood
palette of veins paints tree crimson
leaves depart and trunk truncated
lonely souls restored to life

nailed on tree of heaven's joy
human defects deflected
cross exalted in salad green

Blades in dance
foot on stool pleasingly rests

cutting blade saving grace
surgeon's weapons
piercingly dance

.

The joy of pain comes in our name

tell me who i am muse of my soul
announce my name that i may know
etch my face on mountains bold
paint my eyes on canvas edgeless
talking thoughts in mindful reflection
bear me up rouse me to life
make green my desert sands
set me on ships on shoreless seas
and i'd drink full of joyful pain

The landscape breathes

lost
return to self
externals unwelcoming

air lifeless
escape
fly to skies in storm
humans frolic in exalted filth

minds drink full of deluged darkness
green
a colour arrested
black and grey the daily feast
heart
in solitude congeals
needs awakening on paved roads
mind instructs memory
collapse the pages
don't recount
numbers are nameless

unfit for attention in hapless homes
recoil

be true to self
discover
your strengths
fill
your mettle with marrows incarnadine
breathe
new air from trees you inspire
in the world you create caring and giving
all is aglow lifts the earth
lights the skies

a new age has dawned

externals are fresh
landscape breathes

waiting for a flight
you don't stop evil

or there would be no devil
his powers intact
roams the world seeking to detract

some are fooled into earthly glory

theirs will be a sordid story
the beginning wonderful
all events powerful
wear jewels of passion
fleshly pursuits in fashion
engage in spiritual freedom

drink their content
the waters of wisdom
daring virtues describe their bearing
graces race in formed hearts beating

Time

all time belongs to you
what is time that i should be selfish

placing things here and there
where i want them

assign them permanence
move them change their location
give them a new life
of my own creation
in time

changed the universe

all in a mere calabash
broken into pieces
creation refreshed
in you endlessly joy
i do not come to you

you're waiting my door closed
i see you yet seek you elsewhere
turn my back go places
in my own time

now i know

i come back to you
what's worth more
grains of fleeting joy all good
can't build bricks
nor bricks themselves give grains
of peace when shattered
by timely selfishness
out of time

Where you are

i want to come to you Lord
climbing and twisting to coil around you

the higher i get the more you grow
make me taller that i may gain the light
my roots scratch the surface

yours are driven down
water and food seek life in you
take me by the hand lead me where you are

forever in your garden to sing your solemn praise

You ask me and i say all love

there's no why all boundaries transcended
the heavens dance on a planet one of their own
created by my soul in vanquished pride
beauty streams on with vigour and purity
in unspeakable strength being as God is

all love
self wraps the other

in an expanding universe
all love

Where the light is

darkness everywhere can't see my eyes

eyeless in wild pursuit
my mind flees from me

seeking his presence
memory to the rescue
recalled steep steps to his abode

fall down if i must
even roll
at the threshold there he'll be
to open floodgates of grace
bathe me all over in eternal light

PART II

Of The Soul

The Moon in Seance

A Christmas Kathmandu
>   back from Mass in the cold of morning
>
>   out in the sun from twelve to two
>   return indoors for cheese and crackers,
>   maybe kippers too
>   solar-powered water heated for bath by four
>   all of life is glorious

ordained by Onuora by Ugochi
like Joseph and Mary they give us their best

collapsed into eternity Christmas hearts take flight
seeking new heights wings flapping in fury
to the top of the world Everest capped in snow
low-lying Bethlehem within easy reach
nothing to it like the valley Kathmandu

from the stable the bells summon us
take solar heat to stable cold
to Mary and Joseph
keep Infant Jesus warm
in a Christmas Kathmandu

No greater love than this

can you climb mount Everest
no my Lord i can't

can you swim across the Atlantic
no my Lord i can't

can you walk on water
gosh my Lord i can't

can you fly like a bird
my Lord you're making this test too tough

can you love
yes my Lord i can

do you know what love means
yes my Lord i know what love means
you taught me

and did i not teach you to climb Everest
i don't remember my Lord

what of swimming did i not teach you to swim
i don't remember my Lord
and walk on water did i not teach you that

i have forgotten my Lord

then how do you remember
I taught you to love

'cause my Lord you are here
talking to me
and i to you

Mary and Joseph

the journey was arduous
all the world in the stable
wearing a look unstable
Mary and Joseph walk in anonymous
baby in womb walks out stupendous

Merry Christmas

An advent with Joseph

trudging along your bones astir
go be counted your numbers confirm
our Virgin Mother her womb in dance
as Infant Tenant drums his warm rapture

from door to door you seek out your brothers

no advance notice they all protest
Bethlehem's inn your last resort
no room they swear for census anon
your dilemma compounded any shelter will do

out of the blue you gain a stable
scruffy despoiled unworthy of Master
burdened and broken you make wheat of chaff

and i rush in to give you a hand
my hairs alerted sweep the mangy floor
the stable is warmed my heart's on fire
as pots of my blood put water to boil
garlands of mind create bed for Master

my swaddling skin wraps Him all over
all done to Mary and Joseph race my eyes
flooded with love pouring from Infant's cries

Knocked my socks off

they tell me Lord
write a story
that knocks our socks off

i write and rewrite
and ask myself
will this do it and
knock their socks off

then i wonder
what about you Lord
what would knock your socks off

a cup of water
to one on the cross

a smile from the heart
though you want to knock their heads off

that my son will knock my socks off

Joseph's dilemma

trudging along
your bones astir

go be counted
your numbers confirm
our Virgin Mother
her womb in dance
as infant tenant drums
his warm rapture

from door to door
seek out your brothers
no advance notice
they all say no
Bethlehem's inn
your last resort
no room they swear
for census anon

your dilemma compounded
any shelter will do
out of the blues
you gain a stable
scruffy despoiled
unworthy of the master
burdened and broken
you make wheat of chaff

and i rush in to give you a hand
my hairs alerted
sweep the stolid floor
the stable is warmed my heart's on fire

as pots of my blood put water to boil

garlands of mind create bed for master
my swaddling skin wraps him all over
all done my eyes race to Mary and Joseph
flooded with love from infant's cry

Come to Atlantica

doors seats carpets
floors windows tables
all ordinary things

come to Atlantica
the difference in whirlwind rhythms
sing excellence of human work
all creation in dancing detail

doors open to heavens of love
seats welcome cheerful souls
wearied of languid air
carpets humble pride steps on
floors at the base hold up our faith
sacramental graces pour in through windows
looking out to Our Lord
for the Eucharistic supper
he lays on the table

come to Atlantica
and be whole again

Doors of Atlantica

doors of Atlantica three-inch thick
of finest mansonia
not just a passage but an entry

human person walks to Our Lord
in home at Nazareth

Atlantica doors three inches thick
finest mansonia our forests' gift profound
sublime squares composed on doors
symphonic graces drum on wood
hinge our joys to glory of God
who now bears us into oratory supreme.

Send me a letter

you did not take me out of the world
told me to stay here make it a story
of joy laughter in the rain thunder
in dirt grit commerce sports
be there son then send me a letter
tell me all about it and i'd be thrilled

In what does joy consist

what measures do i use

what intensity
what duration
in what does joy consist

the sight of a rose
the fragrance of a rose
planting a rose
watching it flower
after days of anguish of despair
which gives greater joy
what does greater mean

the cry of a child after birth
full proof of new life born
baby suckling at her mother's breast
a mouthful of lively milk
sitting down unaided back curved
her first walk
suddenly she can run
which is greater joy
 what does greater mean

locked in mystery
joy's ever close ever distant
not understood soon forgotten
till another comes along
it's all a training in being human

to look around and take in
all that we find
not counting not discussing
what has no boundaries
cannot be measured
an airful of joy
we all differ

our character lives in
what gives us joy
heavy rain lightning thunder

romping splashing danger can wait
the beat of the drops rhythm for a song
out with our buckets basins
collect water for a bath
cook our meals wash our plates
drink a mouthful of nature's wondrous joy
parched earth sings its fill
as crops lengthen a glow greener yet
which gives greater joy

in what does joy consist
until we can love perfectly
until we find joy in suffering
joy remains a mystery
who loves so perfectly

but you Mother of Sorrows

Our Lady of the Magnificat
Our Lady by the Cross

Cloak left behind

it's your feast day
today
St. Mark

you ran away
left your cloak
behind

just like you
i run away

leave my poems
behind
naked me

Our own Emmanuel

come i'll make room for you

come with me
and i'll put you in room 101
it's well within your means
and you'd like it
with a view of the temple
to the west
on the east
the river Emmanuel
here's the key
make yourselves at home

there's a fireplace my love
i'll throw in the logs
and heat up the place
make you warm

i get up
move to the roaring fire
all warm and inviting
to the west the temple
yes
to the east...

dear did he say
river Emmanuel is
to the east
i see only trees

a barn

you're right my dear
let's go to the barn
there in the east
we'll have the river of life
floods us with peace and joy
our own Emmanuel
dancing in your womb

He's there in your midst

to Himalaya hurry
huge drums summon our steps
from forests of earthly worries depart
drop all weighty loads
put on your hiking boots
Everest beckons
ascend to heaven home of
The Trinity

angels on guard
bear us on wings of delight
multitudes blend in
form a mammoth crowd
our voices rise
in symphonic celebration
heaven in sight
our hearts race to exhaustion

we've come seeking the Infant One
on pilgrims tickets
Osofisan's theatre of Christmas ecstasy
our identity

we're qualified
we're the chosen ones
africa's voices
all the world sit in our laps
bearing bubbling bags of joy

regret my friends he's not here
the Almighty announces
Infant Second Person of The Trinity
made man is in your midst
in Bethlehem
ensconced in the swaddling cloth you wove
hurry he awaits you
my people of goodwill

Merry Christmas

(Femi Osofisan is a leading Nigerian playwright)

PART III

Of the Spirit

The Moon Said to the Cat

On the road to Awka

on the road to Awka
Enugu long since behind us
with the wheel whirring
the noise unbearing
must find a mechanic
to give us an answer
stopped before vehicles

wrecked in accidents
humanly configured
rusted irons
their souls out of joint
play mangled music
their vibes in disarray
vultures of scrap

fly to the rainbow
drift down in feathers
of hawks resplendent
i step out of the car
in bewildered joy
Answer walks up
in powdery blue jeans

runs the car a while
tightens the screws
with glee he wishes us
safe journey
we drive off in sterling wheels
that hawk their songs
on Awka speedway

Armoured truth

death's demons in cowards concealed
spurt out in bullets seek noble minds
find them well armoured truth their breastplate

famished feeble weapons pierce through
only skin deep they bounce off they flee
season of honour robes knights resistant

for the late Alex Ibru

Pressure is dirt

pressure is dirt
not dirty
the best people work with dirt
know how to recognise it
sometimes ahead of time

the ability to discern what is excellent
runs on the highway of dirt

excellent people
create new dirt
skirt round it seek new lights
shine brighter
working under pressure
to ever step over dirt
dripping in humdrum

corruption is dirty
not dirt

Rain rain it's all rain

from the roof top it drips

drop by speeding drop
a prayer of the skies in dance
swinging bouncing dribbling assurance
huge drums roll out confirm the tryst
 i dance on rumbling pools of liquid love

There's a hat in my hand

deprived not depraved
desired not designed
definite not defined
despoiled not destroyed

a hand in my harrow

Listening to Fifty Cent

running dancing
frenzied transition
the gods in their mansions
peep out in engagement
as casket is mounted on winged trailers flying
readied for bearing to rainbows on heavens
colours transcending in feverish compliance
fill up the arteries and veins with repentance
all that is sordid is basking in brightness
i'm humble in spirit

the soul pleads in judgement
never transgressing the grammar of conduct
honest of purpose corruption a stranger
scoundrels are mongrels thieving a sore
my hands are clean my heart is a palace
nothing untoward can walk through the door
pardon my errors and sins of omission

come in sit down
the gods beat their drums
announce forgiveness for servant repentant
bring up the chalice pour him some wine
feast on his colours with veins overflowing

angels rejoice
proclaim their agreement
announce their thrills the saints welcome a sinner

Tooth and nail

to eat beef
is to eat nails
into spaces between
my gapped teeth

all the fun is gone
flossing does not help
and all i do after
is labour tooth and nail

A thousand worlds one heaven

astounded heart bruised eyes out of sockets
trained on a million worlds in sovereign pockets

the wealth therein seeks freedom from selfish
knights
swords of greed slice daylight joys into weeping
nights

darkness torpedoes our ships of silence
blood gushes from our fruitless patience

a thousand ways to dreams wayward
lost direction songs of charlatans their reward

favours splash on blanched faces
and all that's good flees from crystal places

irokos grow taller for thirsty thieves flying
branches retreat there's nowhere for perching

tired and withered their wings in ashes
eyes out of sockets turn to liquid splashes

a thousand worlds astray do heaven's bidding
strangely rouse sleepless eagles in forests singing

gather then people don't miss your way
rise to the angels in one voice we pray

Dig deep dig down

dig deep dig down a journey to the spirits
through forests of sand
their cries rumbling in the waters

what do you seek they ask
do you seek to drive us off
out of sparkling waters of joy
of restful peace

where do we go from here
what are you doing
free our moorings
send us fleeing to unknown heights

the god of clay eighty foot tall
mighty heavy won't yield to digging
her back spreads out it heaves it sways
her shoulder round and robust
turns our drilling counter-clockwise

press down we must
science puts spirits to flight
why not now
crack
the goddess smash her palace

yea she is broken
clay is empty space created
easy we go but not so fast
god of sandstones asks for whisky

libation is poured to allow free passage
beige bronze brown and red
wondrous in mixture rise to surface
a god is assuaged

penetration deep down
forests yielding
vast gardens of water
can't be reached can't be tapped
we take a rest consult the oracle

twelve yam tubers last year's harvest
one jar of palm wine the morning's best
a basket of eggs not yet cracked
a bevy of virgins freshly hatched

come on this job has to go on
today today we must be done
water must flow or we are dead
our god must bathe and drink her fill

won't naira do the job

now you're talking

i come in various colours
naira has them all
just haul a million and i'd be fine

this job pays us less
no million for you my god
come down to earth rather
rise to the surface
look at our places
you'd agree ten thousand would do

make it a grand fifty
take it or get grounded
no movement no boring
only mere turning to no effect

the sun was paid
the gods all dallied
danced in joy
gave us entry
no sweat all is now water

not so my friends not so
you're in a new world
at two hundred feet
here I hold sway
no sacrifice needed
naira can rest

there's a fair maiden in your midst

her eyes the temple of troy
let me gaze on her
be transfixed
down you can go to
the living waters of life

dressed in chemise organdie
her supple skin
grapes to the lips
there she stands the sun in her eyes
prisms of grace reflected
down down beyond two hundred feet

all the gods in stupor
drunk from her beauty
allow free entrance
three hundred feet below
to depths of sparkling streams

dig deep dig under
water gushes as liquid grace

On desert waves to Himalaya[*]

flooded by the Atlantic rode on desert waves to
Timbuktuwearied breathless coasted down on
mighty Niger
thrown on the beach Onitsha announces Zik of
Africa

on camel back and elephant rides off to
Kathmandureadied for adventure supreme
ascension to Himalaya
morning snow on creation hills caps my hungry eyes

joyously wild the universe to encompass a new feast
of eyes literature on sand-scrolls blown off by strife
fodder for Timbuktu
vaulting ambition faithfully ascending in dreams of
Himalaya
humility voluptuous flows down to valleys a gift of
Niger
canopies rise for country gourmet the chef
Kathmandu
fulfilling birds for salad feast fly from pristine Africa
branches and fronds whisper to mountains reaching

---

[*] *This sestina is owed to my experiences in Kathmandu, Nepal, 2009.*

for Africa

wonders ecstatic find nature's grandeur in whirlwind
eyes for revelry gargantuan a suit of sands adorns
Timbuktu

fresh gaiety cooking kitchen pots thrill Kathmandu
marrying mermaids row in joy on rapid Niger

dancing glaciers nod their obeisance to heaving
Himalaya

laggards lumber to tops and warmth ascends to
cooing Himalaya

Kilimanjaro ballads shoot symphonic romance in
dripping Africa

with trumpets blast bouncing drums float rhythms
of Niger

love dreams climbing séance of souls astonish the
eyes

caravans of dry wines in goatskin bags gift of
Timbuktu

life's rockets rush to bouncing Everest commands
Kathmandu

prizes to mamas and papas by bubbling Kathmandu

hearts of steel from by-gone climbs cooled by
snowy Himalaya

call to mind the grind of mouth-filled sands by
hiking Timbuktu

forests in sorrow shield crackling desert stranger to
virgin Africa

awakened by sunlight ready for sights green are the
eyes
cool waters from springs sprayed by fountains of
Niger
festival's drum images canoes creations by

triumphant Niger
songs verdant and valleys transcending find exultant
Kathmandu
heaven's mansions erect gilded mountains of necks
and eyes
pregnant in prayer saints deliver raptures on tops of
Himalaya
resounding choirs chant choruses resplendent for
waiting Africa
sand hills ecstatic canoes concur it all started here in
Timbuktu

in tributaries triumphant Niger navigates to desert
Timbuktu
and rainbow boats row roving eyes to eager
Himalaya
tempestuous for joy Kathmandu bubbles to
whistling Africa

Eating corn is geography

from north to south they eat their corn
tail to head the earth on its feet
cancer on top

others from south to north
eat their corn from tail to head
the earth on its head
and capricorn on top

latitude

at the equator they start
going round and round spinning the cob
clockwise minus anticlockwise plus
the corn keeps spinning the earth

longitude

Greenwich mean time

eating corn is geography

Ofe Owerri is ready

orchestra sizzling in pot of clay
commands performance of *ugu ukazi*
a symphony simmering in poetic séance
artistic gourmet in creative obeisance
the oracle is summoned for mama's cuisine

blessings in pot a gift of the forest
grant safe entry for hunchback'd stockfish
bearing crayfish on slivers of dry fish
time is ripe palm oil in tenor

announces introit of epiphanies gathering
that all may encounter horizons of union
as self is lost in wholesome offertory
communion arrives bells celebrate

ofe owerri is ready thousands are fed
incandescent joy flows in the veins
the saints exultant dance their hosannas

Cat man dew

you filled my days ticked them off
a century plus six extending your arms
enclose me gather me to your depths
the valley of love increases in this daily cycle
you've trained me to dance through the greens

september arrival in wee hours of morn
heavens drum your glory awaken my soul
angels steer the car to bucolic Latipur
the cactus cackled its welcome our hearts aglow
we pour libations with Nepali moonshine

october to Nagarkot in excitement mountainous
walking and hiking our hearts went racing
downhill we roll to wines on terrace
the sun bids us goodbye and dinner is spread
laughter in friendship all the world's gone feasting

peaks Himalayan command expectant ears
rise stand erect hold your heads high
stretch out your hands tweak our snowy whiskers
to terrace we race goose-pimpled our bodies
solemnly sight God in his majestic mountains

not outdone november spreads its wings
to top of the world angelic hymns ascending

mystery revolving Mount Everest its axis
december in garden Latipur sounds the horn
come my children come my friends

the sun is out sit and behold look up be warm
say your prayers do your readings
i send you back to the forest
no hills no mountains no mirrors
just remember me
i'm your cat-man-dew

Stolen wealth seeks freedom
heaving heart bruised eyes in their sockets

trained on a million worlds in stealing pockets
stolen wealth seeks freedom from selfish knights
swords of greed slice our bleeding nights
vices unbridled sink sorrowing ship of silence
blood gushes from our fruitless patience
a thousand ways to dreams forward
lost direction of charlatans our reward

favours splash on blanched faces
compassion flees from crystal places

irokos grow taller for thirsty thieves flying
branches retreat and there's nowhere for perching
tired and withered their wings in ashes
eyes out of sockets fall on greedy splashes

a thousand worlds of poverty do heaven's bidding
rouse sleepless eagles corruption in forests fleeing
the land is purified freshness is restored
true wealth gains freedom in virtues festooned

Speak

and discover yourself
for in your mistakes
you gain new strengths

shut up
and your mistakes
flow in your bulging veins
pride the heart

make a fool
of yourself
smile in humility
and be lord of your soul

Sentence

escape from self leave carcass behind
fly to words and they'll bear you up
to tree tops of language
a new existence minted
where butterflies speak with the flap of their wings

syllables anew untutored in greenness
flow into leaves and grow greener yet
their voice a symphony in the salad of verbs
and self transforms to nouns in sentence

saps of guavas around idioms frolic

blended with blue they paint pronouns skywards
he in the air and she in the wind
the rainbow advertises on diamonds adverbial

and self transcends to sentence eternal

At twenty feet

at which point do i defer
give him right of way
not make him think i'm defiant
might just push him off
when my blouse worn and torn

would not be scattered
and graze his clean white shirt
when the innocent air

would not be stirred
to inundate his nostrils
with my squalid odour
when my dandruff flaying

would not be guided
to his spotless shoulders
when i would be nothing

nothing to hate
nothing to behold
but an old broken woman

at twenty feet i reckon
i would step into black mud
leave the whitewashed sidewalk
for his anglo-saxon stride

A perfect 10

the score is 9.9
from nine votes
mine a 10 the tenth vote
still score is 9.9
and i wonder

nothing absolutely nothing
would now make it a
perfect 10
let the whole world
vote each a 10 still
it would be 9.99999...
dragging on and on

and i reflected
on the meaning of little things
the littlest of things
and nothingness of 0.0000001
endless zeros
a 1 at the end
and that makes all the difference
no longer zero

still only 1 vote
perchance

made it 9.9

and now all the world
can't make it a
perfect 10

and i smiled

Human greens created
island unto itself this human body
survival its purpose waves greedy conspiring
bruised and battered bloodied in triumph
human surrenders in gamely revival

open up solitude receive the light
that soul secluded selfless may soar
kiss topless trees in thankful trance
forests of humans sublime holy spaces

sun is summoned jungle drums resound
soul steps out seeks partner for dance
green the bodies environments rising
islands transformed human greens created

In maple leaf Canadian

air through stomata in maple leaf Canadian
flows round Brock escarpment custodian
seeks out my soul far across atlantic
The Who rollicking flies revelry gigantic
to Canada i come my spirit dancing
escarpment air floats friends to me singing
wraps my soul in joyful embrace
hearts made one in maple birthplace

Life's equations run in circles

just a little cut the waters assure
the lake at the top we enter a trance
can float and swim our form in balance
the water bores through the bottom
but all is not drained

cymbals announce the bees arrival
honeyed joy in tumult and pain
we rise to graces on heaving hives
silent their fountain
sweetness consumed avarice reigns
masks multiply creation undefined
drum beats of the rainbow

sputter rays effervescent
all is measured
swim to sands on the shore
the grains in poorness congealed

but not for long

share the shore with a new sea
we gain tallness swiftness even
swim to definitions yet undefined
search without knowing

escape get away
seemingly safe
but only an illusion

transfixed in masks
we conjure up visions
of saving joy

in final expression
doubtful
all that's sterling homed in hives

the end in the beginning

Of the Spirit . . The Moon Said to the Cat

PART IV

Of Family . . .
The Moon Curls

In heaven's pearls

sitting here
in the sun
angels in your garden
whisper marvels to my heart
nature's wonders i ponder
in nearby Himalaya

heat renders warmth
in glowing soul
fire blazing a trail
ancestral eagles soaring high
seek new skies rich in history
in towering Himalaya

mountaintops reign supreme
in lowland souls
grassland eyes cannot fathom
farmland too high to till
and houses on slopes dance to tunes
in tumbling stones

my spirit rejoices
in glorious ascent
from Obetiti to Kathmandu
and you, Ugochi, honour from God

your birthday glitters
in heaven's pearls

to my daughter, Ugochi, on her birthday, October 26

Obetiti is where the author was born

Love in the same urn

dad had died and passed on
we have him in an urn
then came mommy's turn
and all's over and done

seventy years they're married
and close together tarried
would be much delighted
if in same urn resided

the undertaker refused
two in urn leaves them confused
each in great joy distinct
embrace God's holy precinct

there's space therein we insist
dad and mom in all consist
one five feet the other no leg
their ash holds grace in egg

hatch God's gift
to give us lift

The mind mines deep jewels

sat next to you at table listening
your character and being poured forth
the oceans of your thoughts
overwhelm worldly desires subdue mountains
a new creation to be revealed
in your boundless mind vast and conquering
whereto will this new spirit run and rest
the race is just beginning
and rest far in the clouds not descended

ascension is the challenge
where is the top what is the top
and top of what your soul in endless pursuit
all the world astounded your genius effervescent
await creation penned at the peak
of human intellect a new world unfolds
where the mind mines deep jewels
and rest grows pearls of love and service
diamonds of your spirit in quiet revelation

To Mass on Christmas day

she leads us lioness in stride
shawl thrown over shoulder
right to left and right again
warmth underneath
pashmina silk sits above all
nestled warmth in firm command
image of power for us to follow

left hand thrusts forward
right hand in blindness
strikes daughter straggling
husband takes two steps

to lioness one
the rest of us in tow
pulled along by donkeyed grandpa
doing his best in humble obedience
to peremptory commands
impassioned leader impatient
awaiting Virgin compassion firing

flies us in to baby Emmanuel

Ma's eyes

my ma's eyes deep and solemn

search the skies o'er the mangoes
ask about the morrow's rainbows
told of storms lightning and rain
gather the sun fan the rays
spread warmth anew that her son may play
and flash a smile on the tearful cloud

Dad and mum live here

what's a beautiful girl like you
doing in a place like this

yes you're right
this place is squalor
i should not be seen here

but why not
dad and mum live here

Your drums will sound

my pa is Right Time
his soul ever ticking
working sweating
each drop a colour
from the Master's brush
in his own good time
he completes the painting
of pa's rollicking life.

a smile is borne
in the womb of the morn
as pa draws me to his chest

order your days son
wait and train
use your brain
in God's own time
your drums will sound
in the market place
in marble halls

Life sends you a card

your childhood years seem distant
like once fitting clothes you've now outgrown
the world's a stranger ever so constant
innocence and purity you stoutly own

your eyes open to a world moving so fast
you run run and don't catch up
it was so easy in years gone by
labour was pancake spread with syrup

life sends you a card with lots of hope
invites you to mountains beyond your borders
filled with courage you climb up the slope
and from the top behold glorious wonders

mind and brain work for the good
heaven's leading light floods your smiling face
soul in hunger seeks Eucharistic food
and now you can run in God's loving grace

My granddaughter Oluchukwu

your name Oluchukwu God's masterpiece
special treasure our souls in peace
twelve weeks pregnant your mom was shot
bullets deflected triumph her lot

here you stand
ten years a woman too young to be so
to look at you radiate the flair
of times dominant your genes on the go

sing a song Oluchukwu
live your dreams with beats suku suku
dance ballet on mom's hearts written
all life's wonders in you proven

to my grand-daughter, Oluchukwu Eseka,
on her 11th birthday, Nov.12, 2009

Papa what do you want me to write

papa what do you want me to write
I'm not in the picture being taken right now

you say pour out your soul
pour out air water sweat
blood soul
let it all flow
you hadn't written a poem before i passed on
now write the undreamt dream vastness
collapsing into sand grains
for new life Mark for new life
write Mark write
beginnings create eternity

ever beginning in timeless space
but where
no compass south glides east and north west
dissolve no form yet topless mountains rise
washed into seas running into rivers
of saving blood from him who makes
grains gain life new breath filling creation
you stand papa irokos all rise bend bow obeisance
pay
and now neck-beaded one bead for one branch

to greet the lovely virgin green forests her prayer
to feed her earthly children
living love trees grow fruits to bear

yield souls for spaceless places by side of
boundless Creator
papa you've taken me to where you are and

brought me back
your gloried beads on my neck to celebrate the
Virgin
who gave us the One his neck on the cross bent

(Mama intervenes)
mama i must bend low to look into your face
never sick never ill ever strong stronger still
faith your breakfast love your dinner
to feed a thousand souls hungry for smiling grace

in you breath of life is manifest
your face from Calabar east to Badagry west
still a being cooking my meal at Emekuku

stomach filled stretches with faith through hope
to love
your pot still cooking invites me to heaven
 your kitchen serving gourmets to Almighty's
delight
all the way to Cana a new marriage feast and you
the chef

No longer fixed in time

graves gravid
immortal
sepulchres spiritual
pictures

portraits of infinity
find expression in
Owerri ballads
flow into depths
lifting your bones
rise

come live in my heart

no longer fixed in time
i descend into yours
since gone

my bones in pursuit
of marrows of time present
bring me back to life
airs bearing you

to boneless tomorrows
flesh you out in new
presents today

so papa and mama
deep prophetic speak
words formed into me
papa running through
verandas of my blood
mama raining waters
on my eyes

My joy of a million saints

the flight to Lagos rescheduled
set back hour after hour four hours in all
fretting exhausted dejected confused

i phoned you thinking you were home

no you were at the airport
waiting
had been there four hours
expectant
don't worry i'm fine i'll wait even longer
till i see your face
what does a father do

how does he feel
joy is just a word

and there are thousands of joys
as there are thousands of saints
all one in God united
each different like none other
Josemaria saint of the ordinary

Augustine of the exquisite
Onyema refinement her signature

united in spirit you extend my soul

i rejoice in your being
exactly as you are
more unneeded
is there more

love minted in the womb
ordinary man in refinement
exquisite that's my son
my joy of a million saints

love from dad

A hope in song

you walk up to meet me
steps brief and fast
don't quite make you out
and then...

i know who you are
that work of God
supreme innocence

surprised the sun breaks out
the rays register on my iris
sweetly embalming not piercing
each a hope in song together a symphony
strings celebrate your childhood
trumpets blast your schooldays
grandfather's joy ascends and i feel

the waters you splashed on my face
baptism triumphant
your sun lifts us for a dance

on Everest
the snow revels in your warmth
and glaciers waltz their way
through greens drumming

beats of babbling bliss
we float in endless exultation

your spirit wells up with adulation
God's masterpiece commanding recreation

Seeing Lulu

a huge moment for me
lost totally lost my old self vanishing
sepulchres erupt in new heavens wrapped
chiffoned angels billowing graces
into old bones new marrows are born

PART V

Of Friends

The Moon Strokes the Candle

blank

My camera says it all

time now time unseen
time standing still and time roaring on
blows as the wind east to west
follows the sun in its ripening brilliance

my camera says it all

morning dew grows petals on brightened brow
supple neck sways to winds of Fela's rhythms
eyes in song dance to dreams drumming
the fragrance of your smile guides me to ecstasy

and the film rolls on in thrilling obeisance

Larry's landscape

bamboo man
the hill he lives on
his heart a mountain
soul grows amongst roses
on clay manured in grace
watered by rains of peace
earned in warmth of rivers
tumbling over stones and thorns
rendered soft and sublime

bent by age limbs slowed by bullets
gait in obeisance to arrows of pain
visible to sight seeking knowledge
of sorrows within
his spirit fresh and firing
energies drawn from morning graces
received in Eucharistic splendour
conveyed to hills of a loving soul

he fills the world with sprinkles of joy
ever rising in solitude springs
spreading to friends in resounding delight
love transcendent in mountainous union

he dreams of towering skies

to reach eternal bliss
ascending joy he lifts his friends
with limbs of gutsy love

In timeless joy

time has meaning only in friendship
for that is when souls are consumed
in the other

time a mystery tiny drops of grace
bathe the soul transforming self
burning bush green in fleshpots
forging vessels wholesomely pure
bear human love boundless in friendship

joy of creation in drums beating
souls truthful their being expansive
gather stories gamely mountainous
retold in time spreading then collapsing
in moments exultant
friends melt in timeless souls

Have you a job now

have you got a job now
fully engaged
bringing in some money
you'd have to ask the wind
blowing in my face

your question fans
embers
of tractors and genius

Children of hope

lilies in crimson joy
rain pollens of gold
on your silken hair

appareled in red
abounding with aplomb
you transfix the assembly

and children of hope
shout their faith
in Abike Dabiri

Seeing Josephine

you bring us a smile
hair flying in grace
marble teeth flashing silence
you step on to walking purity

come then fill us with your love
row our hearts with oars atlantic
the universe gallops on Saharan camels
our ecstasy ascends to Himalayan heavens

parachute down to banana island
your rooftop our landing solace
mansions of peace guide our way
to queenly kitchens of ripened joy

Exquisite Wole

come to Obetiti spread your joy
over our toast in hearty breakfast
the sun pours in frolics in laughter
and water boils your smile the flame
coffee your choice with lumps of grace

come to Obetiti visit the pots
idiom in kitchens of helen's gourmet
created for trojans in Bodija House
sit with me let's pound the yam
your beating heart pestle unto mortar

chunky okro seduces your palate
egusi islands stand up and wave
in *onugbu** rivers flowing in catfish
ofe Owerri queen of buffet
bedecked in pearls of teasing tilapia
announce a feast for St. Raphael's boys
to Obetiti staff club the moon in suspense

wonders what delights await her pleasure
softer she glows and in roundness grows
lights up the garden makes Gulder glitter
your youthful teeth their whiteness flash
cheek to cheek mind spreading to soul
banter and laughter in fulfilling breeze
*Irawo*** creeps out wheels in the cake
and forty candles all rouse and shout
happy birthday exquisite Wole

for Wale Labiran at forty
* a vegetable; staple of Anambra stews
** a student residence in Ibadan
attached to the University of Ibadan

By Pete's pool

here by the pool i sit and stare
solid i'm rock and never a scare
thrilled with rains fired by the sun
come by day and join the fun

some torrid types kick me like a ball
i smile and squirm and watch them fall
friends rub my head and blow me a kiss
i smile and squirm all is bliss

they talk around me their science a blaze
i know it all just stuff my ear
lipids and structures with sculptors in tow
knock me to form displayed for show

i smile and squirm by pete's pool i breathe
airs of joy for membranes on guard

Kilimanjaro

a mountain in wonder lost to himself
juices transcendent spill over his face
the stage succumbs in venous amazement
surges through arteries creation astir

Kilimanjaro in urgent desire
seeks expression in theatres volcanic
foundation grounded in grasses of blood
swirls and dances to Femi's heartbeat.

for Femi Osofisan, who is Kilimnajaro

Kwame

geared in red in iroko stance
from shoulder to toe truth in séance
rasta wig tickles the neck
idioms in whispers caress his soul

theatre of arts spreads wide its arms
louvers of love embrace the singing wind
lights in gold forge a lustrous crown
create a frame flaming in fame
preface done Kwame commands

pipes and drums and flutes and gongs
giants collide and housegirls slip through
virtue's confirmed steels Femi in truth

For 'Femi Osofisan

Pheromone's my name

there they sat
all the world their canvas
stories to paint lives their colours
forests and trees flush in red
bleed sap of denuded trunks
unto gardens freewheeling in love
hibiscus yellows gardenia's blanched

not to worry let's leave the forest
fold the canvas head to Paul's[*] abyss
fashion a riddance for itchy nuisance
make insects swarm to inviting pheromones
and pests are caught on sticky sheets

great parent you are
your brood now protected
mosquitoes are banished

pheromone's my name
i'm always in charge
soft and silent

Paul University, Awka, Anambra State

Connected

sitting on the terrace
our hearts flow to you
friendship festooned in crystal brilliance
our minds marvel in sublime exultation
pour out their treasures in torrents tumultuous
our lives on canvas in colours conducive
spread out before you in humour magnetic
we breathe the air of Shitra in concert

A place a people

quiet serene in valley Kathmandu
idyllic setting in coolness of morn
breathing spaces in arms reaching out
gather harvests of patient tasks

the sun dials at noon of day
speed our hearts to dazzling grace
captured in fields on hills inviting
yield harvests of lives fulfilled

humans in place their hearts aglow
race to districts flooded with pain
partner persuaded a friend assisted
woman is periled yet triumphant

our souls transcendent to Indira we fly
nest on treetops on mountains ascendant
she gathers her brood humans in despair
lifts their spirits to heights unmeasured

Losing self

losing self in that stealthy space
where contemplation
migrates to distraction
and mind expands
to envelope the universe
then collapses into
caves in deep seas
losing self discovering self

where the ending din
of the market place
greets the glorious glow
of moonlit stances

where devil peeps in to tempt
tries to stir thoughts of
things worldly
then is chased away by
angels of light

human person adrift
lands on shores of
revealed truths

Turn left at Abakpa junction[*]

the instructions were clear
to him they were
to me a meander in a maze
turn left at Abakpa junction

bear right to en-en-pee-cee

en is fine

as in *en ville*
but en then en again
is a sentence to enlivened dreams
pee i won't get into
cee see you've got it
Lord that i may see

Chiedum sees and directs further
approaching fly-over take right
continue right to the end

well here i am the fly-over to my left
i flew over now headed toward Port-Harcourt

please sir get back turn around
and head to Enugu

my car is stiff and stubborn
with a one-way mind
can't turn steers toward truth only
i cajoled love songs in tow
please turn my speeding sweet
we must return to Enugu
voila, success

continued on the right road
Okpara statue to the left
Government House on the right
poor Nigerians stranded and strapped
between powers that soothe or crush
Okpara the old of virtues long since gone
stands tall in monuments noble and caring
but now no one cares
the new the modern wears you thin
saps you dry
vices fight for space in your soul
robbers to your right
please sir i did not say vices

i said nice place
Ugwuoma is a nice place
and i didn't say robbers, sir
i said Robert as in Robert de Niro Robert Browning

now sir continue to Metropole hotel
and you'll see the Air Force Primary School
to your left we're just down the road
going down anywhere isn't my forte

in the frenzy i passed everything

where are you now sir

i'm uphill somewhere

i mean sir just follow the Air Force road
and we're at the end of it

Air Force road he tells me
he lives at the end of the runway
i just flew over a fly-over
now must force the air to lift me up

Lord here i am at Ugwuoma House
they say it's a good Hill
a happy ascendance to meet you in the clouds
and you've been waiting for me
sorry Lord

my director leads me with his Chi
'God leads me' that's Chiedum
then Lord make him fly
give him wings to bear
his massive frame fat belly and all
as he announces

it's Communion time
forty mansions on the mountain
built to last on the bread of life
come live with me

turn left at Abakpa junction
and let's build more mansions
year after year as we march on
to the palace of our Father.

happy birthday Chiedum
(my God leads me)

* *following directions to Ugwuoma House, Enugu*

Boneless tomorrows

graves immortal sepulchres scriptural
paint portraits of eternity spiritual
rivers of joy from gardens in embrace
flow into depths lifting their bones

airs bear souls of my fathers
to boneless tomorrows
depths prophetic announce new moons
flesh them out in new todays

alive they arise no longer fixed in time
ascend into years long since gone
my bones in pursuit seek marrows of time
the present into yesterdays now live in me

Printed in the United States
By Bookmasters